FIRESIDE SERIES Vol. 2 No. 2

MW00463271

A Master's
Key for
Manipulating
Time

A MASTER'S KEY
FOR MANIPULATING TIME

ISBN # 1-57873-064-3

JZK Publishing
A Division of JZK, Inc.

P.O. Box 1210
Yelm, Washington 98597
360.458.5201
800.347.0439
www.ramtha.com
www.jzkpublishing.com

These series of teachings are designed for all the students of the Great Work who love the teachings of the Ram.

It is suggested that you create an ideal learning environment for study and contemplation.

Light your fireplace and get cozy. Prepare yourself. Open your mind to learn and be genius.

FOREWORD TO THE NEW EDITION

The Fireside Series Collection Library is an ongoing library of the hottest topics of interest taught by Ramtha. These series of teachings are designed for all the students of the Great Work who love the teachings of the Ram. This library collection is also intended as a continuing learning tool for the students of Ramtha's School of Enlightenment and for everyone interested and familiar with Ramtha's teachings. In the last three decades Ramtha has continuously and methodically deepened and expanded his exposition of the nature of reality and its practical application through various disciplines. It is assumed by the publisher that the reader has attended a Beginning Retreat or workshop through Ramtha's School of Enlightenment or is at least familiar with Ramtha's instruction to his beginning class of students. This required information for beginning students is found in Ramtha: A Beginner's Guide to Creating Reality, Third Ed. (Yelm: JZK Publishing, a division of JZK, Inc., 2004).

We have included in the Fireside Series a glossary of some of the basic concepts used by Ramtha so the reader can become familiarized with these teachings. We have also included a brief introduction of Ramtha by JZ Knight that describes how all this began. Enjoy your learning and contemplation.

Contents

INTRODUCTION TO RAMTHA
BY JZ KNIGHT

"In other words, his whole point of focus is to come here and to teach you to be extraordinary."

You don't have to stand for me. My name is JZ Knight and I am the rightful owner of this body, and welcome to Ramtha's school, and sit down. Thank you.

So we will start out by saying that Ramtha and I are two different people, beings. We have a common reality point and that is usually my body. I am a lot different than he is. Though we sort of look the same, we really don't look the same.

What do I say? Let's see. All of my life, ever since I was a little person, I have heard voices in my head and I have seen wonderful things that to me in my life were normal. And I was fortunate enough to have a family or a mother who was a very psychic human being, who sort of never condemned what it was that I was seeing. And I had wonderful experiences all my life, but the most important experience was that I had this deep and profound love for God, and there was a part of me that understood what that was. Later in my life I went to church and I tried to understand God from the viewpoint of religious doctrine and had a lot of difficulty with that because it was sort of in conflict with what I felt and what I knew.

Ramtha has been a part of my life ever since I was born, but I didn't know who he was and I didn't know what he was, only that there was a wonderful force that walked with me, and when I was in trouble — and had a lot of pain in my life growing up — that I always had extraordinary experiences with this being who would talk to me. And I could hear him as clearly as I can hear you if we were to have a conversation. And he helped me to understand a lot of things in my life that were sort of beyond the normal scope of what someone would give someone as advice.

It wasn't until 1977 that he appeared to me in my kitchen on a Sunday afternoon as I was making pyramids with my husband at that time, because we were into dehydrating food and we were into hiking and backpacking and all that stuff. And so I put one of these ridiculous things on my head, and at the other end of my kitchen this wonderful apparition appeared that was seven feet tall and glittery and beautiful and stark. You just don't expect at 2:30 in the afternoon that this is going to appear in your kitchen. No one is ever prepared for that. And so Ramtha at that time really made his appearance known to me.

The first thing I said to him — and I don't know where this comes from — was that "You are so beautiful. Who are you?"

And he has a smile like the sun. He is extraordinarily handsome. And he said, "My name is Ramtha the Enlightened One, and I have come to help you over the ditch." Being the simple person that I am, my immediate reaction was to look at the floor because I thought maybe something had happened to the floor, or the bomb was being dropped; I didn't know.

And it was that day forward that he became a constant in my life. And during the year of 1977 a lot of interesting things happened, to say the least. My two younger children at that time got to meet Ramtha and got to experience some incredible phenomena, as well as my husband.

Later that year, after teaching me and having some difficulty telling me what he was and me understanding, one day he said to me, "I am going to send you a runner that will bring you a set of books, and you read them because then you will know what I am." And those books were called the *Life and Teaching of the Masters of the Far East* (DeVorss & Co. Publishers, 1964). And so I read them and I began to understand that Ramtha was one of those beings, in a way. And that sort of took me out of the are-you-the-devil-or-are-you-God sort of category that was plaguing me at the time.

And after I got to understand him, he spent long, long

moments walking into my living room, all seven feet of this beautiful being making himself comfortable on my couch, sitting down and talking to me and teaching me. And what I didn't realize at that particular time was he already knew all the things I was going to ask and he already knew how to answer them. But I didn't know that he knew that.

So he patiently since 1977 has dealt with me in a manner by allowing me to question not his authenticity but things about myself as God, teaching me, catching me when I would get caught up in dogma or get caught up in limitation, catching me just in time and teaching me and walking me through that. And I always said, "You know, you are so patient. You know, I think it is wonderful that you are so patient." And he would just smile and say that he is 35,000 years old, what else can you do in that period of time? So it wasn't really until about ten years ago that I realized that he already knew what I was going to ask and that is why he was so patient. But as the grand teacher that he is, he allowed me the opportunity to address these issues in myself and then gave me the grace to speak to me in a way that was not presumptuous but in a way, as a true teacher would, that would allow me to come to realizations on my own.

Channeling Ramtha since late 1979 has been an experience, because how do you dress your body for — Ram is seven feet tall and he wears two robes that I have always seen him in. Even though they are the same robe, they are really beautiful so you never get tired of seeing them. The inner robe is snow white and goes all the way down to where I presume his feet are, and then he has an overrobe that is beautiful purple. But you should understand that I have really looked at the material on these robes and it is not really material. It is sort of like light. And though the light has a transparency to them, there is an understanding that what he is wearing has a reality to it.

Ramtha's face is cinnamon-colored skin, and that is the best way I can describe it. It is not really brown and it is not really white and it is not really red; it is sort of a blending of that. And he has very deep black eyes that can look into you and you know you are being looked into. He has eyebrows that look like wings of a bird that come high on his brow. He has a very square jaw and a beautiful mouth, and when he smiles you know that you are in heaven. He has long, long hands, long fingers that he uses very eloquently to demonstrate his thought.

Well, imagine then how after he taught me to get out of my body by actually pulling me out and throwing me in the tunnel, and hitting the wall of light, bouncing back, and realizing my kids were home from school and I just got through doing breakfast dishes, that getting used to missing time on this plane was really difficult, and I didn't understand what I was doing and where I was going. So we had a lot of practice sessions.

You can imagine if he walked up to you and yanked you right out of your body and threw you up to the ceiling and said now what does that view look like, and then throwing you in a tunnel — and perhaps the best way to describe it is it is a black hole into the next level — and being flung through this tunnel and hitting this white wall and having amnesia. And you have to understand, I mean, he did this to me at ten o'clock in the morning and when I came back off of the white wall it was 4:30. So I had a real problem in trying to adjust with the time that was missing here. So we had a long time in teaching me how to do that, and it was fun and frolic and absolutely terrifying at moments.

But what he was getting me ready to do was to teach me something that I had already agreed to prior to this incarnation, and that my destiny in this life was not just to marry and to have children and to do well in life but to overcome the adversity to let what was previously planned happen, and that happening including an extraordinary consciousness, which he is.

Trying to dress my body for Ramtha was a joke. I didn't

know what to do. The first time we had a channeling session I wore heels and a skirt and, you know, I thought I was going to church. So you can imagine, if you have got a little time to study him, how he would appear dressed up in a business suit with heels on, which he has never walked in in his life.

But I guess the point that I want to tell you is that it is really difficult to talk to people — and perhaps someday I will get to do that with you, and understanding that you have gotten to meet Ramtha and know his mind and know his love and know his power — and how to understand that I am not him, and though I am working diligently on it, that we are two separate beings and that when you talk to me in this body, you are talking to me and not him. And sometimes over the past decade or so, that has been a great challenge to me in the public media because people don't understand how it is possible that a human being can be endowed with a divine mind and yet be separate from it.

So I wanted you to know that although you see Ramtha out here in my body, it is my body, but he doesn't look anything like this. But his appearance in the body doesn't lessen the magnitude of who and what he is. And you should also know that when we do talk, when you start asking me about things that he said, I may not have a clue about what you are talking about because when I leave my body in a few minutes, I am gone to a whole other time and another place that I don't have cognizant memory of. And however long he spends with you today, to me that will maybe be about five minutes or three minutes, and when I come back to my body, this whole time of this whole day has passed and I wasn't a part of it. And I didn't hear what he said to you and I don't know what he did out here. When I come back, my body is exhausted and it is hard to get up the stairs sometimes to change to make myself more presentable for what the day is bringing me, or what is left of the day.

You should also understand as beginning students, one thing that became really obvious over the years, that he has shown me a lot of wonderful things that I suppose people who have never gotten to see them couldn't even dream of in their wildest dreams. And I have seen the twenty-third universe and I have met extraordinary beings and I have seen life come and go. I have watched generations be born and live and pass in a matter of moments. I have been exposed to historical events to help me to understand better what it was I needed to know. I have been allowed to walk beside my body in other lifetimes and watch how I was and who I was, and I have been allowed to see the other side of death. So these are cherished and privileged opportunities that somewhere in my life I earned the right to have them in my life. To speak of them to other people is, in a way, disenchanting because it is difficult to convey to people who have never been to those places what it is. And I try my best as a storyteller to tell them and still fall short of it.

But I know that the reason that he works with his students the way that he does is because also Ramtha never wants to overshadow any of you. In other words, his whole point of focus is to come here and to teach you to be extraordinary; he already is. And it is not about him producing phenomena. If he told you he was going to send you runners, you are going to get them big time. It is not about him doing tricks in front of you; that is not what he is. Those are tools of an avatar that is still a guru that needs to be worshiped, and that is not the case with him.

So what will happen is he will teach you and cultivate you and allow you to create the phenomenon, and you will be able to do that. And then one day when you are able to manifest on cue and you are able to leave your body and you are able to love, when it is to the human interest impossible to do that, one day he will walk right out here in your life because you are ready to share what he is. And what he is is simply what you are going to become. And until then he is diligent, patient, all-knowing, and all-understanding of everything that we need to know in order to learn to be that.

And the one thing I can say to you is that if you are interested in what you have heard in his presentation, and you are starting to love him even though you can't see him, that is a good sign because it means that what was important in you was your soul urging you to unfold in this lifetime. And it may be against your neuronet. Your personality can argue with you and debate with you, but you are going to learn that that sort of logic is really transparent when the soul urges you onto an experience.

And I can just say that if this is what you want to do, you are going to have to exercise patience and focus and you are going to have to do the work. And the work in the beginning is very hard. But if you have the tenacity to stay with it, then one day I can tell you that this teacher is going to turn you inside out. And one day you will be able to do all the remarkable things that in myth and legend that the masters that you have heard of have the capacity to do. You will be able to do them because that is the journey. And ultimately that ability is singularly the reality of a God awakening in human form.

Now that is my journey and it has been my journey all of my life. And if it wasn't important and if it wasn't what it was, I certainly wouldn't be living in oblivion most of the year for the sake of having a few people come and have a New Age experience. This is far greater than a New Age experience. And I should also say that it is far more important than the ability to meditate or the ability to do yoga. It is about changing consciousness all through our lives on every point and to be able to unhinge and unlimit our minds so that we can be all we can be.

You should also know that what I have learned is we can only demonstrate what we are capable of demonstrating. And if you would say, well, what is blocking me from doing that, the only block that we have is our lack to surrender, our ability to surrender, our ability to allow, and our ability to support ourself even in the face of our own neurological or neuronet doubt. If you can support yourself through doubt, then you will make the breakthrough because that is the only block that stands in your way. And one day you are going to do all these things and get to see all the things that I have seen and been allowed to see.

So I just wanted to come out here and show you that I exist and that I love what I do and that I hope that you are learning from this teacher and, more importantly, I hope you continue with it.

— *JZ Knight*

A View from the Other Side

Greetings, my beautiful masters. I salute you from the Lord God of my being to the Lord God of your being, and welcome back. Let's have a drink. Beautiful, beautiful, beautiful.

O my beloved God,
I am on the march.
I am learning
more intently
of my origins,
my power,
and my purpose.
O my beloved God,
I have gathered here
with kindred Spirits
to develop more
this my march.
I say to you,
whatsoever
I focus upon,
I accept.
And, O my God,
rent the veil
that separates me
from that which you are,
forever
and ever
and ever.
So be it.
To life.

We had a roll call of nations one day, and they were from everywhere except here. And despite that which is termed language barrier and cultural barrier, they felt at home here, and they understood and they did the work superbly. And never did I have to run them out of latrines or hiding in the bush or in their automachine, because they came too far and they went through too much. They were true pilgrims, and always the true pilgrim is the one who will lay down his humanity for the sake of his learning.

Now this year in your time there have been several of your students pass this plane, and they passed this plane with dignity and courage, dignity and courage. But those that passed were already on their way, that their illness had become integral in their thinking. And try as they may, they made great effort but, you see, the effort, as it were, becomes the wisdom on the other side. And I want you to know there is not one of my people that get out of that body forever that I don't meet, and they have all met me, and I them. And to their great and wonderful astonishment, I do exist. And there was no fear; there was only undescribable love. And they laid down those corrupted, diseased bodies. And there was not one of them who was bruised spiritually, and this is what we want to work for.

And in their review, I was with them at their review. And we laughed, and they cried and I laughed, because when it was over, when all of their energy had passed and they saw where they could have done better and they saw what they had damaged in others in their life, and to their wonderful amazement had come to great peace, a few, two precisely, still held onto the suffering of their bodies and blame for other people, but they got to see that and got to understand that suffering is not an infliction by others. It is an acceptance by the sufferer. And they got to understand that, and when they did, that was all that needed be released.

So as their drama played out — and I want you to know — every card they made, they got to see that card and they got to watch themselves in the field and they got to watch their dreams in the field, and they got to watch, as an added bonus, what that thinking created as potentials for them, which no one else gets to see. That was superb, because they have an opportunity to accept those potentials, if they wish to come back as wisdom and get to live them out in the next lifetime.

Now what all got to see, that none other has ever seen, is their greatest desire was not to see their God, because their God was present, but to see one vast nothing. And so we erased the screen and brought forth the window and they got to move into the Void. That is sublime. You cannot comprehend altogether that which is termed infinity with really the mind of man, because his capacity to envision it is constrained with his own definition of limitations. But what is the Void? And they all got to experience it. They all got to go back to Point Zero, something that one day I will look forward to doing with you as well.

I want you to know that they are studying more. They are in a great Retreat. And what are they studying? They are studying the books of their own limitation, the laws that they contrived here, and what they were not able to get beyond. It is not a hard study, not with their preparation. And they have been invited to look in on you this week, and I am certain that you may see some of them because this is the great school that they loved and understand its significance.

Now having spoken this to you, here is something you should understand, that we are, you and I, a most rare group. We are rare in the sense that it is very hard for the human to be God, it is very hard, because the human senses take control, because they have never been used properly or learned properly in how to be experienced in making known the unknown. It is very hard. So as many of you who have traveled back here, no matter your excuses, it speaks greatly of you, and you should know that, that this school is not a hard school. What I teach is not hard because, you see, you already have it in you. What is hard is the fight between your humanity and your divinity. That is what makes all of this hard.

To have you come back and to work here in the Spirit of one group is marvelous, is beautiful. It is beautiful because every time we labor in the fields of God we make a difference in your life. Some of you, it is a difference that lasts five minutes, and maybe out of this whole Retreat only five minutes is going to be changed in you. Now I should like a lot more than that, but if all you can spare in surrender is five minutes, I will take it. But in the five minutes, as it were, you become changed in understanding and compassion and vision, and this makes a marked difference in your own life. Maybe we have softened the edge of criticism. Where before your criticism had sharp and defined edges, perhaps the five minutes you learned here, as an example, sharpened and curved them because you needed that for you. Our ultimate criticism is always to ourself. And so when you got to be more forgiving of yourself, then you find that when you leave here, that is carried over in a reality. The reality is expanded because of that, and so the sharp edges are softened to everyone you go back to.

Now that is a blessing, people. That is a blessing. It is not something that people try to do; it is something that should come naturally. And the only way that we spring naturally from ourself is when we have owned it ourself. To be any other way is to be artificial and contrived. To be naturally God is what we are all here to aspire for — not artificially God, conveniently God, because it makes great conversation, or seduction, or because it makes you look lofty; that is contrived — naturally; it simply is the essence of the entity. That is what we want to do.

Now that makes a difference. If you die and you go to where your fellow students have already gone, you will see that five minutes in your life, and your soul will rejoice; your Spirit will rejoice. What will make you sad is to see where you were too lazy, too human to be bothered with anything else. That will make you utterly sad because you can see how easy it was to just simply give up the prejudice against self. And in giving them up is called surrender, and in their place comes beauty; it flowers. Then it is natural. The five minutes you will celebrate on the other side.

**IN THE LIGHT OF ALL ETERNITY,
WHAT IS THIS MOMENT WORTH?**

Now my daughter I taught a very important saying to that helped her greatly through many turbulent times, and I tell you this, the same thing. When you are doing something or talking about someone or you are in the midst of it and you are being challenged, the instinct is to go back to your humanity, the past, and rebel from that place. But I said to her, "Daughter, in the light of all eternity, what is this moment worth to you?" A wonderful gauge, because when she asked herself that, she had two choices. She could make a choice for this life and for the moment to appease the moment, or she could make a choice in the light of all eternity that no matter in the light of all eternity, when reviewed upon, that there would be dignity and nobleness and joy in that decision, no matter how hard it was here. And I want you to learn the same process. In the light of all eternity, what is this moment worth? Now that is the learning of a true master, a true master in the skin of a human being, because that skin can get very thick, and it can do many things to try to survive and compromise its values, its nobility, its fairness for the sake of a moment. But that moment will last all eternity.

Well, this is what I want to say to you. You have brothers and sisters who have passed and they all have dealt with what you are dealing with now, all of them — you are not unique — and they will never do it your way again. But yours is the test because now you have the opportunity and the knowledge to live forever in this body and you never have to die. And it is already in you. And what is going to turn the mechanism on is it being natural in you, and the only way that we bring about a natural acceptance is by mastering the lack of attitudes that prevent us from that acceptance.

We are privileged, you and I, but you and I are based upon a dream I had a long time ago. And in the light of all eternity, I am dreaming that dream now, 35,000 years ago, because I have the vision to see now what I could not see as a common man, dreamed into being. So now you should know that this is a rare event and they will not always be, and give yourself the pleasure of acknowledging that you made it here and that it was important enough for you to come back.

Now what I also want you to look at: Did you come back because it was required of you and because what would your friends think of you if you weren't here — well, if you can bear to look at that, I want you to — or are you here because your soul and your Spirit have inspired you to be here, because there should be no other place in the world but here? And you are going to need to complicate that a little bit with excuses, but I want you to get rid of them and just ask yourself that question because if you do, then you will know how far you are going to learn at this event and how far you aren't going to learn at this event. If you don't want to be here, because you have to be here, you are not going to do very well, and maybe we are only going to get five minutes of inspiration and surrender out of you. But those of you who want to be here, you will grow magnanimously.

I want you all, when you make this transcendence to transcend this plane, I want you to be my warriors of old and my masters of new, and that you are worthy and you have the courage to look at everything in your life — there is nothing sacred; there are no sacred lies — and those of you who choose to stay, that you are going to stay here and make a difference, and you are going to have to press through personal prejudices and laziness and attitudes to get there. It is worth the journey.

You should also know that this is not a religious event — one should never separate one's Spirit from everyday life because without the Spirit, there is no everyday life — and that you shouldn't be here because this is your religious obligation. If you think in those terms, you will never gain the benefit from this school that is really being offered here. I am endeavoring to transform you from weak, self-centered, ignorant, abusive, selfish, surviving people. I am endeavoring to transform you into what is already there: an absolutely outrageous, unlimited, manifesting human being empowered solely by the holy Holy Spirit.

And what does that mean? I am not preparing you for monasteries and I am not preparing you to be missionaries. I am not preparing you to be ascetics and live in the mountains away from all humanity. I am not preparing you to live in rags. It is not as if you have to give up anything worthwhile. You are giving up nothing that compares to what you are going to get. I want you to have everything, because only until we address the utter lack of everything are you going to be masters and it won't own you anymore.

I am not preparing you to be spiritual people. I am preparing you to be Gods — there is a difference — and I intend for you to live richly, beautifully, and powerfully. I prepare you to go out in the world and to enjoy what you have never enjoyed before and have the power to do it. You think you are having a good life now? You have got a boring life, boring. Do you think that laying someone every other night is exciting? Do you think that going to discos is exciting? You think that getting a few new one-hundred-percent-cottons is exciting? Then you are a cheap date, cheap. What are you missing? Is that it?

Now when you learn this, you don't have to worry about money because you will learn the power to reach in your pocket and pull it out. You don't have to worry about one hundred percent cotton. Let's do something really outrageous; let's weave some light in one hundred percent polyester. You are going to learn how to do it. And who wants to date someone on this plane? The twenty-third universe has serpentine beauties there. Why not have an evening with a God?

Here is the point. The point is this schooling is not about being a martyr. Oh, no, I was never a martyr and never should you want to be one either. It is a limited, lousy place to be. The only way you are is dead? That is the only place you are is good? No, I want you to be a powerful people. I want you to know that there is a truth in quantum mechanics, that the Observer is responsible for reality. Now what kind of reality? Well, that is equal to what the Observer thinks. And if the Observer is thinking it is not possible, then no possible reality happens, and that is the reality. Do you understand? I want you to know that you can hold out your hand and manifest it in there. I do want you to know you can put your hand in your pocket and you will have greenbacks or "redbacks" or gold, you can have anything, because there is no law preventing you from having it. So that is the great message.

When you are a master of this school, you can dine with masters. When you are master of this school, you do not have to wait for an aeroplane to take you here; you can be here in a moment. Is this possible? So possible it is frightening. How long will it take? Well, how long do you think?

I am here to teach you this is not about being a religious person. It is about being God, the ultimate experience, and being able to have the power to own it all and to do all of those things that you only have half dreams about, so that one day this isn't important any longer. You understand? Then we will go on. We can never go on if this is pulling you. Do you understand? So I am not oblivious to your needs. I am not oblivious to your sense of authority and sovereignty. They all come with what I am teaching you. So I want you to know you are not wasting your time being a monk here. You are going to be fabulous in every aspect of your countenance, and your standard will fly greatly in your bands, and you will have a communion with the great ones, not mediocrity. Do you understand?

If you know that then, change your attitude about this work. See it first that it is encouraging and giving of knowledge that allows acceptance that allows materiality, that it is the encouragement to live forever in the same body, that it encourages you to define wealth in the moment, and in the next moment if you don't want it, you can define it. But it gives you choices, which God should be all about. It gives you the opportunity to be young and old or in-between, and it gives you the option to be sick or well, whatever you wish. But you should be a master of all of them. And everything that comes your way you should experience until you can master it, because that adds to the bounty of your perspective as the Observer. Do you understand? How many of you understand?

So don't come thinking you have missed anything. You have missed squat. You come here knowing that you are going to learn the art, to the greatest of your ability, how to manipulate energy fields and how to manipulate them into your life, with the knowledge to understand the process. And with that you should have all ears open, full attention, and full participation. That should eliminate this aspect that you have to be here. That should say, "I want to be here, because I am going to get everything when I do."

Now you can sit here and argue for your limitations. You can argue and say, "Well, I haven't done so well yet," but, you know, you didn't listen very well either and you didn't participate with utter surrender. You participated with resentment. You think you should have all of it now without any evolution involved. That is not how it works. You are supposed to have everything but you are supposed to experience it all, and that is like the stairways to heaven. Every experience enriches the next step, allows us to see the next step, to envision it so it can manifest, and we keep moving up from there.

If you have accepted your state of attitudes, then woe is you because you will have partaken of the kingdom of heaven from its crumbs and not its bounty. And what are we going to say when you come to the light? Well, you were just too tired or it wasn't acceptable or you didn't make time for it? What kind of excuse is that going to be in the light of all eternity? And who would logically rationalize you don't have time to participate and learn the skills of being a manifesting God? You don't have time for that?

That is what I want to teach you, the Boktau Group. It is possible to get anything you want. There is nothing that says you can't have it, I swear to you, and the only one that will argue why you can't will be you.

So we are going to work diligently and with full participation on the concept of lack and all of its broadest avenues — lack of participation, lack of motivation, lack of desire — and in that lack we get the excuses of rebellion. And we are going to obliterate it and work for the ultimate prize, the manifested end, the acceptance to the manifested end. They need a clear brain to do that, a clear body to do that. And attitude is everything. Moreover, I want you healed. I want you healed. It is attitude.

Dissolutionment — The Art of Metamorphosis

So what about those days that are the yawning silence of emptiness where all of the predators of lack start to snap at your heels? What about those days when nothing is happening with your manifestation? What are those days? I will tell you what they are. The caterpillar is in that cocoon and he only becomes dissolved when he no longer thinks as a caterpillar, because he must think as a caterpillar to recoagulate himself. And when you don't think as a caterpillar for the days you are in a cocoon, your body dissolves. If you don't get sleep in forty-eight to seventy hours, your body starts to dissolve, so you have to dream dreams to re-form it. If the caterpillar doesn't think about a caterpillar any longer, his body dissolves, and so will yours. What happens when the caterpillar's body is dissolving? So is his reality. What is his reality? Being earthbound to limbs, eating green leaves, and being fed upon by predators. He is vulnerable. But when he no longer is the caterpillar and he doesn't dream it or think it, he dissolves his body. It is a natural fact. So with that he dissolves then that which is termed the propensity of being in the reality of the caterpillar, and he starts to dream about the butterfly.

Now here is what you should know about your manifestations. When you keep working on them and focusing on them rather than your lack, what will happen is they will dissolve and so will your reality that is involved in the lack. It too will dissolve.

Now there is a time when the body dissolves into a thick, dark green, blackish gel. See this as the dark night of the soul. And why is that? See that when you no longer think in lack, when you are no longer punished, when you no longer are craving the former life and you don't think that way, then you dissolve too and so does your reality that is involved in it. Now there comes the place in dissolution: In dissolution, nothing happens; everything is melted. What is important is that you are in a mid-state, a hanging state. And because you are ignorant and you don't know any better — and we are trying to change that — there is a panic that sets in. There is the state of no-state. That is the state of dissolutionment. Are you listening to me? Just like in nature, it is that way before it re-forms.

Now here is what you haven't learned yet, that in order to be the God, you must melt away the human. In order to be fabulously wealthy, you must melt away fabulously lack. In order to have anything, you must melt away the former, and we do that by thinking only of what we wish to be and no longer what we were. And that must be a continuous constant. And I have taught you how to do that with the List that is long and time-consuming.[1] There is a reason for it to be long and time-consuming. I have taught you that with the discipline of focus. I have taught you that with cards. I have taught you how to keep staying in the state of I Am, waiting for dissolutionment.

Dissolutionment says that you have walked out there and you are falling off the cliff, nothing is happening — nothing is happening — and you get afraid, because in that fear your humanity wants you to retreat and recoagulate, recoagulate your past thinking. How many of you understand? "Go back and start thinking rationally." That is what it says to you. "Give up. This is nothing but a dream. It has put you in harm's way." What is the worst that can happen to you? It wants you to go backwards. That is sort of like the caterpillar in a state of dissolutionment feeling a little free-flowing and getting nervous about that because he has dreamed about the butterfly but he isn't a butterfly yet; he can feel he is

---

1 See the glossary as well as the appendix in *Changing the Timeline of Our Destiny*, Fireside Series, Vol. 1, No. 2 ed. (Yelm: JZK Publishing, a division of JZK, Inc., 2001), pp. 61-66.

nothing. Now wouldn't that make you a little frightened? That would be like the caterpillar saying, "Well, this is not a state I like; it is too weird," so he starts thinking about what he used to do, and so then the coagulation goes back to being the caterpillar. How many of you understand that? So he just recoagulates the past, doesn't he, instead of going forward with becoming the dream.

In your life there is going to be a pause. And every one of you calls that the testing period but, you know, there is nobody that really tests you. You are God, and this is not about a test. Humans think it is a test because they think in terms of punishment and failure. This isn't a test. This is the quiet. And in that moment of no-place we are given the options to go forward with the dream that brings forth the butterfly or we can go backwards because we need that security, and we go back and think the way we used to think because at least there was a security in that.

I have taught you all that the brain loves habits. No matter what they are, it loves habits. No matter how destructive they are, the brain loves habits because habits are a dependable state of sovereignty. They are dependable. Habits are more dependable than husbands and wives. Do you understand that? That is why you go back and do them, because they are predictable.

Your humanity has to be broadened to the point that it understands it is in a no-place and that it will not go backwards and pick up habits because it is a state of security. How many of you understand that? But you have to stay in the no-place. Picture in your mind that there is a dissolving going on — are you listening? — a dissolving going on. Now think of it in this way. Before the butterfly can emerge, there is complete dissolutionment of the caterpillar, except the caterpillar's brain and its Spirit. The brain becomes transformed when it thinks only in terms of butterfly then, because that is the dream. The dream is the new neuronet. So the old that has to be thought about every day isn't thought about anymore, and so it dissolves.

Think about it this way. You are not being tested; you are in a state of dissolutionment. And if you keep going backwards and trying to recoagulate your former attitudes, the longer that state is going to stay — how many of you understand? — because you are going to go back and try to recoagulate a past thinking while everything is trying to dissolve. It is called lumpy dissolutionment, lumpy stuff.

Now that is easily provable in biogenetics because if you take two diverse species and you put them together, you are going to come out with a creature that resembles both of them. So that is no different than having a creation that you are still carrying a coagulation of lack with. It is going to be a very bizarre creature. It will be the sort of creation that more than likely you will feel you never deserve, because that is going backwards along with the abundance. How many of you understand that? So be it.

Now the teaching to focus upon that lack but remove people, places, things, times, and events — wake up — let's see the brilliance in that teaching now. We dissolve the past by removing people, places, things, times, and events. When we focus on lack and then remove lack and make it stand on its own without any neuronet reference point, just lack, it cannot stay, so it dissolves. And in that moment we place what it is you want, and we place it there without people, places, things, times, and events. How many of you understand now? So the dissolutionment is very pure; it is not contaminated. And that is how those who apply this righteously find that card. And the teaching here is if you can do it on the field, you do it in life.

You are not being tested. You are spanning an abyss of transformation. At any point you can turn around and go backwards. That is your choice. The ones who have the grit go forward in spite of it all and hold that dream, and if everything dissolves, it will be re-formed into the butterfly on the other side. And you have to hold that dream without people, places, things, times, and events. That means that the dream must be dreamed pure butterfly with no semblance of a caterpillar. And the only way we get a butterfly is to dream it without any connection to the former reality. Now that is what you are going to be working on.

Now some of you would call that faith; you are having faith that your dream will be. You don't have to do that. You don't have to do that. Are you in this school for the long haul, as some of you have said? Are you marching? If you are here for the long haul, you know that this teaching has profound ramifications not only in this lifetime but all lifetimes to come, and that it is here we meet the nemesis of lack and it is here that we meet the nemesis of the necromancer in us. This is the true conquering of self. How much will and how much warrior do you have in you? This is where the warrior that has lain latent rises up and comes alive. This is the courage to transform. What does that mean? That means that some of you when you are dissolving will panic, be frightened, depressed, as you call it, and will be having nothing but nightmares of people, places, things, times, and events, and they will be on you like a marching army because you invite them in. They are familiar. That is why you invite them in — they are familiar — because then you narrowly escape losing everything.

Now there are some of you that are pure materialists in here, pure altered-egoists. You are still in school; amazing. You think only of what other people think about you and you have trashed the teachings in the outer world for the sake of that. Now there are those of you who will never do that, not in this lifetime, because what people think about you is too damn important. It is more important than becoming the butterfly, so you do it with smoke and mirrors, or whatever else you call it, illusions. And you look like you are changing, but you haven't got what it takes to change. And you won't ever do that because you are not willing to let everything dissolve to re-form the new because you are too afraid. And what are you afraid of? What people are going to think. And why is that important?

Because the brain is there to keep the body surviving, and those people are important for food on the table and shelter over your heads and food in your belly. That is what it comes down to. Now we see what is the root of all of this. It is the human, the weak, transient human. It is said, and it is true, flesh and blood may not ever enter the kingdom of heaven. And they are flesh and blood and therefore they can never go where you go. And who made them that way? They made them that way. They made a choice. That is all it is, is a seductive, sacred lie. And there are others, but what does it matter? The dream is more important than the backlash of criticism.

Now we have a Christ in the making. We have a true master rising from the ashes because in their opinion, in the light of all eternity, the decision to dream is the law of God, and that is their only destiny. And in the light of all eternity, to make that choice for change may for a period cause havoc, criticism, may even cause war. That is not punishment; that is dissolutionment. It will all be over soon, because then the dream will recoagulate into the butterfly and you can fly away and leave your neighbors.

For those of us who are sincere, as it was in my life and I am desirous that it is in yours — that this life is not about holding status quo — we are here to change; we are here to dissolve the old and dream the new. And that is what this is about, especially if you are concerned with the light of all eternity. And if you are, it means much more than the physical presentation in this lifetime. It means what do we do with our choices here. And should we regard ourselves a lesser creature than the lowly caterpillar? If you can't change, then the caterpillar should be worshiped by you, because they have the courage to dissolve it all.

So that lull, think of the former dissolving. How long does it take? Well, it is always up to you. When is the day that you wake up and you don't care and it can all dissolve? That day will be the day you will re-form into what you want to be. But every step of the way, remember, you are the one that puts the chains on. And you put the chains on in your mind — you put the chains on — and it is you who hold you back, no one else. That is liberating.

WE REARRANGE THE PAST
EVERY TIME WE MANIFEST

Now if I was to review with you what I have said earlier about you are not going to be religious people but you are going to be Gods, that is the ultimate, then who gets to be that? Well, you all do, according to your choice. But I will have students in here — because it is already seen — I have students in here that will lay it all on the line without regret, resentment, blame, or victimization. And there will be a cold wind blow through their soul, but they will form into the light of the school and a light of the world. And they see that they have lost nothing except what was and what they have already been to gain it.

Not everybody is ready to do that. So how about those of you who aren't? Well, you will do it in small degrees. You will do it in degrees that allow you to do it in your comfort zone, and you will change little bitty pieces, five minutes. That will help everyone. If you just do five minutes' worth, you will help the world. But on the other side of that you are still your material self. You haven't really gone to the heart of it, and so you will be able to do some things but you are not going to be able to do it all. And you will be in awe of those that will be, and you will say, "You are incredible," because you will know the truth. "I could never have done that." And you are right; you could never have done it.

The group is a group on a mission, and that mission is to be the metamorphosis realized. And that is my mission. And every step of the way is attitude; it determines your performance.

So we are going to have work to where we are learning the art of liberation. We will learn how subtly we hold onto things. We are going to see it for ourself, and we make the choice on which we wish to do with that. And you get to do it in the quiet of your work, and you just keep remembering people, places, things, times, and events, what is holding me back. And you are working with that attitude.

You must understand what you create in your life does not come from anyone else's energy. If it does, it is connected to people, places, things, times, and events. And if it is their energy, who is in charge of their energy? They are. Are you? No. What you are going to get is going to be made out of your energy.

Think about this: The butterfly was made from the same substance that the caterpillar was made from, yet they look like two different creatures. Your reality will be made from the substance of your energy. That is why the way that a master creates reality within a moment is because it is not dependent upon anyone else, people, places, things, times, or events. So where does the magic come from? Himself. Where does the marvel come from? From his energy. When he is so free from the attachment of people, places, things, times, and events, when he is so free and liberates himself from such constraints, he has at will in a moment the power to manifest whatever he wants from himself because there is nothing blocking him. And what can he manifest from himself? The mind of God, that is what. Now doesn't that make logic to you? Did you really think that we were going to teleport, as someone said earlier, Japanese watches from Japan to manifest them in the field? What manufacturer did we rob to get them here? No, we don't do that. It is much more complicated than that and much more simpler than that. We rearrange the past every time we manifest, every time we manifest.

You never take a pot of gold out of Fort Knox. That would be robbery. But anytime you want to manifest gold that has got a minted mark on it that is acceptable as currency, then you are rearranging the past and your involvement in past events that happened thirty, forty, fifty years ago, and suddenly you are going to live an event that brings you that gold. And all the history books will be rewritten, and one day you will open up and see that you are one of the people involved in it. Of course you didn't know that now because it is yet to be rewritten.

There is much more to understand but it is safe enough to know that dreams should not include any people, places, things, times, and events. It should never be based in them. It should simply be based that it is pure of what it is and uncorrupted, and there it comes quickly. But it must have a state of dissolutionment to where all of those attachments can be pulled away, because if it is re-formed you will be enslaved with it to other people, places, times, and events. How many of you understand? So be it.

Now think of this: When you learn this, one day your land will be paid off. And how do we know that? Because you are not manifesting new land; you are manifesting your land. And how do we know that is your land? Because you can go down to the title company and it will be in your name and you have owned it for fifteen years. When the present moment is dictated, the past and future are dictated. If we endeavor to move back to the past, then we take the past and we bring it to the present. If the past occupies the present, it contaminates the future with its past. How many of you understand what I am saying? If we take the future and put it in the present, the future is never accepted as the present. Whatever is future in the present will always manifest future. In other words, the future will always be manifesting. And what does the future mean? That which is not yet. Even when you see your dream, in a future tense you have attached to a time. And that is the one thing I also said: Do not put to your dream people, places, things, times, and events. "Times" is not just backwards; it is forwards.

Now we want to clear to where when we are analogical in the present moment that our present is not contaminated with the past, people, places, things, times, and events. In other words, you get rid of your lack back here, which you are going to work on today, that causes a state of unworthiness — and you are going to have to address that — so that the dream can sit here, and we have to get rid of people, places, things, times, and events in the future. What we want cannot be dependent upon any of those items.

So then that begs the question then is this even possible? Very possible, because if we can put in the frontal lobe the dream completely without interference, then what happens is evolution is occupying the present moment; the dreamer is occupying the present moment. That is the wisdom of the caterpillar who is occupying the present moment and not rerememembering the caterpillar but dreaming the dream in the moment of the butterfly as his reality dissolves around him. Then the art of Now is all that exists. And if the art of Now exists in the present, the present contaminates the past as well as what? (Audience: The future.) That is right.

That is why it is so hard to describe time to you because, you see, time is based upon the moment. Time must have a point of measurement before it can be concluded as time. And to a master and all ascended beings, time is contained within the present. When the dream is dreamt righteously, it changes the past and the future.

So now if the dream is that your land is yours, if your dream is that you are fabulously wealthy, this is how it works. If that is the dream without contamination and it is worked on and held, when it appears it will change the past; you will have always been the owner of that land. Furthermore, you paid a handsome price to those people that you bought it from, because there is no bargaining in God. It just is. You will have always owned it. So that then occupies the future as well. That is your future.

Fabulous wealth, so how are you going to explain this to everyone? Well, because you will have already gotten it and everyone will know that you have always had it. This is how I and my fellows think, because the future is right now and so is the past right now. Don't you know that in the paradox I told you I am right now dreaming this future, don't you understand what I was saying? I have created this future out of the ashes of the past and they are happening at the same moment. And there are those of you in this same moment that are gathered in the encampment below, this same moment. And every moment, every moment, it is all changing.

So for those of you who think that this knowledge is worth having, then this is the work for you. And the only thing that it suggests is that you need to have the knowledge, full participation, and apply what you have learned, and the results will show themselves. And you will know when you are in a state of dissolutionment. You will also know when you go backwards. That is the teaching. You should know this. But you also should know that when you are the master of it, you will have always been the master of it.

So how many of you understand now a bit better about all your potentials existing simultaneously? How many of you understand that? When I tell you your dream is already existing as a potential, do you have now an understanding of how that could be? Because whenever we elect the moment and are full throttle on the moment, full passion, full involvement, when we are fully there, when we are fully righteously it, then that is the potential that always was. The past is changed. How many of you see that?

That is why there is no excuse for being a victim and there is no excuse to stay unhealthy. There is already a reality that you are already healthy. There is already a reality that you are younger. There is already a reality that you are wealthier. There is already a reality that you are a genius. There is already a reality that you are liberated. And there is already a reality that you are a full-blown God. It already exists. We just have to address the present with this wisdom that I am endeavoring to impart to you that won't come until you participate and understand it fully. Got it?

Now this is our agenda, to learn the experience of what I have taught you this morning, to broaden your ability to accept. And if it is intriguing to you to understand that, the concept of the moment, you can understand that simply, you will understand the impact of what focus without any limitation has on past and future potentials. It is a marvelous thought. It is the way the universe works. You understand that we are going to work on that righteous focus without people, places, things, times, and events, and you are going to learn what those are because you will have to deal with them, and that is past and future, and learn what it is to simply be in the moment with a creation and know completely and utterly what the caterpillar and butterfly know and what is the secret of their metamorphosis. It is very simple. You are going to learn then the art of manifestation, and you are going to move up a degree from feathers and paper clips to something a little more substantial, along with broadening your acceptance. More than anything, you are going to change, even if it is for five minutes.

You stay in the moment, you do everything I ask you to do and, more importantly, surrender, surrender. If you have a monkey-mind going on, get your sword out and hack its head off. If you have an attitude, you conquer it. If you feel bad, you heal it. If you are feeling like a victim, you hang them and be done with it. Got it?

Time Travel: Changing the Past and the Future

Now turn to your partner, who will now be your partner, embrace them, and explain to them what you understood about your contemplation of all times now being present.

So how many of you worshiped the belief that the past was set and could not be changed? Raise your hands. It is all right to confess in this audience. Well, you can certainly look at your own life and say, well, things haven't changed much.

Now here is what I want to say to you. That is a belief system based in ignorance. But here is the danger about that belief system, is that you never have a future. That is the danger. And also the other danger is if you believe that the past is unchangeable, then you will never be one of those splendid few who have the opportunity to change it because it will be a law in your reality not to participate.

Now, masters, now I have taught you many outrageous things and you are sort of getting to a point now that nothing can top the last outrageous thing. I like that because what it means is that you are very broad up here. I want to broaden you because the more broad that you are, the greater the reality you are going to experience. Do you understand? So now what have you got to lose to believe that the past is changeable? What have you got to lose? The past. If you don't have this knowledge, how can you experience it? God only knows what you know.

The reason why, to a splendid few, extraordinary experience occurs — that they cannot explain what they saw, what they experienced, moreover, how they felt — is because they were unprepared for the experience so they gained nothing from it. Generally speaking, the extraordinary doesn't happen to the ordinary. Only ordinary happens to ordinary.

So the way that Point Zero was created was that the Void contemplated itself. Well, contemplation then is the first principal law. That means that God sprang from contemplation, and if God sprang from contemplation, then contemplation must be the point of expansion. So I give you information that I want you to contemplate on. Your playtime, as you term it, is just as valuable as your schooltime, and in those moments that are quite ordinary is when you should be contemplating the extraordinary.

So now beings, the Gods, extraterrestrial beings — whatever those are — they have the capacity to go back in time and change all of the future. They did. So is it possible that there was a past that was different than the past you know now? Yes. Well, they have the ability to do that. Now wouldn't it also come to knowledge with you and to logic that if then time travel is possible, then it has everything to do about the occupation of the present? It isn't that anyone goes backwards. It is that backwards is brought forward to Now. How many of you understand?

So herein then lies some other observations that I want you to at least have a philosophical and theoretical knowledge base about, and I don't want you to go to sleep. If that means then that history can be changed, if it means then that your own personal history can be changed, if that can be altered, then what about world history; can that be changed? Is it possible somewhere that there never was World War I, II, -Two and a half, -Two and three-quarters? Is that possible? It is. Quite a concept, isn't it? Now you know why you are only familiar with the one history? Because that is the one everyone agrees upon and keeps reaffirming. Yes.

Now here is something else I want you to pay attention to. If thought is coagulated energy, then the way that we change that which is termed the past is to dissolve it like the caterpillar does its former body, and out of the liquid arises the butterfly. Now how do we do that? We abolish any attachment to the past, that there is no past in the present; there is only the moment and what is occupying the frontal lobe.

Something else I want you to understand is that whatever occupies the frontal lobe is the key from contemplation, and from contemplation brings forth the pattern for energy to collapse into. So then this means that unless we reaffirm a new present, unless we do that we continuously reaffirm the past and that is the only present we will ever know. And how do we do that? You would say, "Well, I didn't do anything to make my life so terrible," but you do, because you keep thinking about it. Your neuronet is a program that runs in front of a great screen and the screen is called the frontal lobe, and that frontal lobe, whatever is projected there — whatever is projected there — is collapsing energy in your future into the Now. What do you think you are held together with? A reaffirmation of what you think you are, a reaffirmation of what you think you are.

So a very wise and astute entity would say, "Could this be the reason there were mantras?" Yes, because what was the mantra about? The mantra wasn't about idle chattering. And could this be what repetitive prayer was about? Absolutely. What was it about before it became a dogma? It was a prayer to reorient the present to a specific will and, by doing so, dissolving the past and re-forming it according to that will. What would be the logic behind primitive repetitive prayer and what would be the logic behind repetitive primitive chanting if not for a whole period keep the frontal lobe occupied on a specific dream? How many of you understand? So be it.

Now here is what I want you to remember. If you are held together by a program up here, a neuronet program, that must continuously run in order to hold the status quo together, then who designed the program, and what would happen if the program was dissolved and a new one put in? Would reality change? Absolutely would. So now what does that say? That says that there is divine plan to this, that while we occupy these bodies we must have a subconscious program set in place that continuously is reaffirming this body, because if we don't, the body will dissolve on us. Your subconscious knows that. That is why it puts you to sleep. It has to put you to sleep in order to dream dreams that communicate with the body to give it the law of reestablishment. That is why only ten minutes of sleep, you feel refreshed. The brain must have that in order to recoagulate you.

Haven't you ever seen anyone that has gone without sleep for forty-eight hours? Have you ever looked at their face? Does it look like it is melting? Doesn't it feel like it is melting? It does. It is. The tiny, the tiny, which is the atomic structures, are moving back into energy. They are turning to thickness. Ever notice how fatigue brings on thick matter in the eyes, thickness in the saliva? What do you think that is from? Why should it be there? The tiny is dissolving. That is why the brain puts you to sleep, in order to reaffirm the tiny. You don't see the destruction of the tiny at first because all you are used to looking at is whole patterns, whole objects. But when they start to get blurred is when they are losing their form. They are being dissolved from within.

So if we created that program, which we did, to hold together this body, which we did, and we programmed in genetically perpetual memory to reaffirm our status, then what does that say to you? The Observer must be on duty to keep reality fixed; correct? Now wake up and think with me. If that is so, that describes why we have a mystery called sleep and why it is needed, but that should also say to you something about the nature of the power of who you are. And the very, very smart in this world know that and use it to their advantage.

THE MASTER'S KEY:
OVERLAYING THE MENTAL PICTURE

So then we come down then to the ability to manipulate energy. Your past is only as long as your bandwidth. There is nothing that exists outside of that bandwidth. There is one vast nothing out there. The illusion is you think you can see beyond it. You can't. You are agreeing with other bands. The past then doesn't really exist except up here,[2] doesn't it?

Now think about this. The training of that which is termed the villager to transmute them into the master is to teach them that when we set a table and nothing is on it and we ask a villager is the table bountiful or empty, villagers always see it as what? (Audience: Empty.) and think that the only way they can make it bountiful is mass to mass. Got it? The student in training to be a master will say it is abundant. And the two will look at each other, and the villager, incredulous, looking at the master, saying, "There is nothing there."

And the master says, "But that is what you choose to see," and the master overlays onto the material the vision of abundance. And when we take the material world and we take the mental world and we put them together, we have the new picture forming of reality. So which one of these is going to have abundance in their life? (Audience: The master.) Louder. Always. That is the training.

What is the temptation? The temptation is to go back to the intellectual brain, but what does it know? It only knows the past, and that is not a lot. And it fights to have its opinion recognized and it will argue that there is nothing there. Nothing like arguing for your limitations, I say. The master reprograms that and works on it to change it. Now

2 In the brain.

don't go to sleep. I am endeavoring to explain to you the miraculous in simple terms so everyone here gets it.

So when you wake up in the morning, your first thoughts fix the day, don't they? How many of you agree? Your first thoughts fix yourself, don't they? How many of you agree? Absolutely correct. How many of you woke up feeling fine until you started worrying? You fixed that, didn't you?

So the study then of the Great Work is to manipulate reality and evolve it. You should never settle for an empty table. It should always be seen as abundant. And we should never settle for lack because lack in any form brings about complacency, laziness, and reinforces the past and the way you think.

So, people, if the body must be put to sleep in order for the brain to reprogram the cells, according to their nature, to form and reconstruct the human, then every single day you must be thinking in order to reaffirm your present, your reality. And if the only way and the only mechanism that you have been thinking with is your neocortex, your past, that which is termed the neuronet up here, the intellectual entity, if that has become the supreme God forming reality, then your midbrain is taking that and casting that forward, and your past is not only your present but it is your future. If the neocortex is your God, you are in trouble because energy will only stay coagulated according to the message it carries. Now it is a particle that carried a message. Here is consciousness inextricably combined with energy to its collapsing point. It collapses because that is what it is supposed to do. It carries the information to collapse. We think it should collapse. If we don't reaffirm it, what happens to it? It goes back into free space. It carries no information on it; it is free energy.

So this then formed the caterpillar, but if that caterpillar does not continue to recognize its nature, its nature is going to dissolve. This is the gel. And it is about right here that the dream started riding the energy, and then it re-formed. This particle carries the message of transformation, but it is the same particle that was over here. Do you understand? It is important you understand because if you don't have the knowledge, you won't accept what we are going to do. We don't have to get more energy. We just have to trade in the old, dissolve it, and we will have all the energy we want. How many of you understand that?

So now here is something else that is remarkable. If this is the past right here, that particle must be reaffirmed every day. That is why we have attitudes. When we no longer focus on the past — here is the key — we focus on a dream that is not connected with people, places, things, times, and events. That is the key to liberation because, you see, this particle and this energy is encumbered with consciousness. That consciousness is a neuronet, a plan, an attitude. If we were to dream about the butterfly and then carry this old attitude, what would happen? Louder. We wouldn't dissolve. You have got to have this unencumbered before the dream can re-form.

So now here was the teaching. People, places, things, times, and events, they are all key to the program of the past. When we create new without any of the above, we are liberating the energy from the past and re-forming it into the new. As long as it is attached to people, places, things, times, and events, it will never be liberated. It will always carry the virus of attitude.

Now logic this, reason this: The neuronet is the personality — is the personality — is the sum total of the events culminated in your life. That neuronet is based in lack. And why? Because it has never recorded the events thus far of complete, unlimited mastership, has it? So why would you seek the advice of your memory in regard to your fabulous wealth? That is sort of like taking counsel with a pig, which a lot of people do. That is the way that the great ones look at you. No, not as pigs, although there are some who think you are tasty. Why — they look at you — would you decipher your future based upon the integrity of your past? Why should your personality have dominion over your dreams? Now don't you think that is a noble question? It is. But here is the way that it is, that teaching you to be a master inevitably gets jaded by the personality because it analyzes it to death — it analyzes it to death — and puts a stronghold onto the moment, and it is all based in analytical opinion. It is all based in past experience that has nothing to do with a fully realized, masterful mind. It has nothing to do with it. Well, how small must you get in order to meet smallness on its own territory? Very small.

Now if this is your passion, if this work, the Great Work, is the greatest work going on in your life tonight, then you have to ask yourself, "Is it going on in my life? Am I making the effort to understand the knowledge that is being imparted to me, contemplating it, and then utilizing it? If this is about me, then it is I am the alchemist as well as the base metal, and it is I who must light the fire in my own crucible, and it is I who must be melted down to be re-formed. I am the alchemist."

So here is what I want you to know. If you are a passionate steward of the Great Work, then you must be willing to look at the way that you think, not with that which is termed destruction but to look at it for the way that you think, that you are wholly without an opinion on the future because you are based entirely in the past. And you should never accept your past thinking to override your dream of the future. That means your past thinking should not corrupt this moment and that it should be allowed to be pure for the dream so that the dream can then manifest from the energy of the past.

How do you know that you are going to have a miracle? Well, you have been a miracle every day of your life because every day you have been reaffirmed. That is a miracle. You don't know it because you are busy being it. And it is not until we change the modus operandi do we see a slight fluctuation and difference in your life. Then we call that miraculous. But the truth is you have been reaffirming who you are every day. Your choices for reaffirmation have been the limited mind.

There is a reason that great beings create their day. There is a reason for that master walking out on the roof of the world and dropping his saffron robe and sitting in his loincloth in a cold beyond comprehension, because he is one with life and dares to be one with life and he has created that he is creating reality.[3] And his test is can he do that, and he does it every morning.

Great ones know that the day is depending upon them, reality is depending upon which side of the brain they choose to affirm it with, which part of them they wish to affirm it with. Great ones create life, and we leave no footprints. What does that mean? We have dissolved our past. What does that mean? We are no longer that; we are this.[4] Do you understand? And we want to dissolve the past because only in the dissolutionment of the past can we be formed as immortals. The caterpillar cannot become the butterfly if it reaffirms, while it is in the cocoon, that it keeps thinking about yesterday and it keeps thinking about tomorrow based on yesterday's opinion. It cannot form the dream. It must abandon itself. It must abandon its past, and that nothing else exists except the dream of what will be. Then that particle can now dissolve back into energy and the new dream will create itself out of the gel, out of the energy.

We don't want a past. Every great master knows that, every student of the Great Work who is worth his salt knows that, that in order to have the fabulous kingdoms that are existing a hand away we must be willing to be nothing of what we were and everything of what we want to be. And we must learn the discipline of understanding how to do that. We create reality. It doesn't just happen.

---

3 See "A New Day on Terra at the Roof of the World" in *A Master's Reflection on the History of Humanity, Part II, Rediscovering the Pearl of Ancient Wisdom* (Yelm: JZK Publishing, a division of JZK, Inc., 2002).
4 A master.

Listen, you don't want to be crippled, and no matter how glamorous it is to have these infirmities, you don't want them because they stand in the way of radiant immortality. And I don't care how pitiful and wretched your childhood was, don't you know how many childhoods you have had? When is enough enough? I don't care; dissolve it. It doesn't exist and it shouldn't have any echoes onto this moment. The past is the past. The events are the events. The people of the past — past itself is time — and all of the things must be abandoned. They are abandoned in the frontal lobe intentionally. They will then dissolve and the new will be formed. From that rebirth occurs.

It Takes Twenty-One Days to Change the Neuronet

So now do you know that every moment of your day you are reaffirming that moment, you are reaffirming your life? And with what information are you reaffirming it? Social consciousness. Why are you worried? What is there to worry about, holding things together? Isn't that hypocritical to what you say you want? Isn't what you want to be liberated and empowered? Then why are you trying to hold things together? Doing so infringes upon your right for abundance and liberation.

The yellow brain is a lacking brain, it just is, and it is an ugly one. It can excuse its thoughts in the most deliberate and cunning of ways because it is there to make you survive. The yellow brain has never known the future; it only knows the past.

So how many of you know how many days it takes for a caterpillar to go through the metamorphosis in a cocoon? How many? It takes twenty-one days for the human being, twenty-one days of continual focus, to change the neuronet. It takes twenty-one days of continuously living a dream as Now before it is accepted in total dissolutionment. Now that is for the normal person, but most of them can't do it for twenty-one days because getting up early and creating your morning for twenty-one days is just beautiful in the beginning and noble, but after a while it gets boring and tedious and you get tired of talking about that which your yellow brain is arguing is not. So most students never make it to twenty-one days of continual dream acceptance to a point of utter dissolutionment. So they try it for a week, they don't see any results, they give it up. And why do they give it up? Because the yellow brain argues with them that nothing is happening. While the yellow brain has got the stand arguing, it is arguing for your limitations. It is reaffirming them.

Now as I said earlier to you, today in your time as you know it, is that you are not here to learn to be monastic, religious creatures. You are here to learn to be God and in that to go back to the original principle, to make known the unknown. That is what we are here to do, not reaffirm the known. So change is fearful to the yellow brain because it does not know what lies on the other side of it, and it is important for it to know that for its survival. But when you know that that is how it works, you will pay no mind to it. You will not give it mind. You will understand that change is elemental and it is necessary, and it is what we are here to do. To change means to dissolve the old and refabricate it into a new, not reaffirm the old.

Now it also means a rather large and important step in the Great Work. It means that gold can come from lead, it can come from tin, it can come from dirt. It means that Cinderella's carriage came from a pumpkin. It means that the white horses came from white mice. How many of you understand? It means the beautiful garment came from her garment of rags.[5]

---

5 See *When Fairy Tales Do Come True*, Fireside Series, Vol. 3, No. 1 ed. (Yelm: JZK Publishing, a division of JZK, Inc., 2003).

Learning to Move into the Midbrain

So this is what the new lesson is about. Now that I have taught you that we can change the past by changing the present, then what you are going to learn to do now is — you have done very well at manifesting mass to mass — now you are going to learn to manifest from the ashes of the past, and that means the energy, your path. Your path, you are walking in a bubble, a teardrop, and it is a funny house of mirrors because it gives you the illusion that there is much further than there really is, but there isn't. You are walking around in a bubble of energy and everyone agrees upon what everyone sees. That is why it is important everyone think alike. When everyone thinks alike there is an unbroken chain of reality, a large vista, as it were. When everyone agrees, we get what someone wants. Your bubble of energy contains all of the worlds known and unknown, and your bubble of energy here is responsible for holding everything together. Energy, energy, without it you wouldn't be here; deliberate design through thought.

So now I want to teach you why it is so wonderful not to have a past. I want to teach you to manifest without the commentary of the yellow brain, of people learning to manifest without people, to manifest without a place, to manifest without other things, to manifest without an event, a happening, a drawing, a bingo, a luck, time, to manifest without the need for time. When we eliminate all of that, we have only the moment, virgin, pure Void. And in that moment all the energy is free space because when we remove all of these, we no longer have lack. We have no lack. We know that this incorporates it. When we remove it we have none, and that is free space. The free space then has the ability to mold quickly to whatever you want.

And how do you know you are going to get it? Because it is coming out of your energy field. And how do you know it will be on your path? Because your path is coming out of your energy field. They are both the same thing. So you are not going to miss it, and no one is going to take it away from you, and you are not going to not see it. It is going to be there because it is coming out of you. How many of you understand? Got that?

Now this is a discipline worthy of study and participation and patience. It is not that it doesn't work. It always works. It is working now. What we need to do is to train on which part of the brain to move. We create it with the yellow brain but we don't want its opinion. We move to the midbrain, the art of sending-and-receiving, what I taught you to do. The art of sending is to be able to send the message without the opinion of the yellow brain. The midbrain is a giant antenna into the future, and whatever is going to be cast in the future is a reflection to the past. We cannot create the future without ultimately changing the past. We are throwing ourselves upstream.

So the art to manifesting in a moment is the art of training oneself to know how to move from analytical thinking to no thinking. The midbrain doesn't think. You should know that. It is incapable of analytical judgment. The midbrain, the psychic brain, does not judge; only the intellectual neocortex does. The midbrain is sending and receiving. It is the antenna, the broadcaster.

Learning to move to the midbrain is simply accomplished when we focus on the object. We see the object being there in spite of any person, any place. It is not going to be at any particular place; it is unattached to a place. And it is unattached to another thing that is going to make it happen, and it is unattached to an event. If we can still hold it and know that it is, even without time — it is not going to happen in any time — when we remove time, we give it our full present. When we can do that, we have literally removed the opinion and the neuronet of the yellow brain, and it immediately goes midbrain. Now it is broadcasting. That is what is going to reaffirm the future-Now.

Now a wonderful teaching in this little sentence, and it says "Ask and ye shall receive." Ask and ye shall receive. Now what is miraculous about this teaching is that usually people when they are having difficulties are trying to figure out the difficulty. How many of you now understand what that means, trying to figure out the difficulty? So who is figuring it out? (Audience: The yellow brain.) And what experience does the yellow brain have? (Audience: The past.) Now also in trying to figure out, you scheme and plan and try to be clever, and now who is doing that? So all the while it is trying to find a solution to the problem, and it will go to all ends to try to solve it because it has got an image to live up to — how many of you understand? — and it reaffirms that image all the time.

Well, what is so profound about the statement, "Ask and ye shall receive"? Because those who finally ask have acknowledged that they do not possess the known solution. And it is a surrender. It is a surrender. It is sort of like "I give up. I cannot figure this out. I give it up. I need help." That is when you go to your God and say, "I give this to you. I don't know what to do." That is wonderful. You should have done that a long time ago — how many of you understand? — because if you would do exactly that, you would move out of occupying the neocortex and you would move into the midbrain. "I need help. I am not getting it up here." Then it always comes, because when you no longer have the solution and you no longer have the answer and you are no longer clever enough to figure it out, then your God will. But don't you think that it should have been done a long time ago?

So suffering is unnecessary, always has been. It is unnecessary. But suffering does make martyrs, which also can help reinforce the victim. How many of you understand?

Now surrendering is not about getting drunk, no. That makes you merry, but that has its own problems. It is about just saying, "You know, I want this, and I in my experience do not know how to get it. I am asking your help because

I don't know, and I don't want to stand in the way. I don't want to be in the way of my own greatness." And those who ask will receive. Simple, eh?

The Alchemist's Crucible

So here is what I want you to do. I want you to make a card. And we have learned that one of the processes in this school is coagulating a model of reality, and we do that on cards. We have all sort of learned to accept that this is how we model reality. And it is a splendid way to do it, and it is a lot less time-consuming than doing it on clay tablets or hides.

So now I want you to use your yellow brain and I want you to select from the pool of its memory an object that you would like to manifest that is a step up from a feather, a paper clip, a wisp of down, something a little more, more, more substantive, an object. And I want you to color that object and to be able to see that object three-dimensionally in your brain so when you are drawing it, you can move all the way around it, see it bottom, top, and inside. I want you to be able to do that. But you draw the picture and color it because that is the object you are going to work on. And it is going to bait your yellow brain because it came from your yellow brain, but the bait means that we are going to cull it from the yellow brain but we are not going to ask its opinion. And here is the true training. The training is the yellow brain will try to figure out how it is going to happen but you say, "No people are going to give this to me, and I am not going to expect it at any place either, and I don't want any event to cause it to happen, and I don't want this at any time. And I don't want anything close; I want this." So what is your yellow brain going to do with those orders? You have just eliminated every possible opinion.

When you do that correctly and then learn to focus on it, which we will do after we have made the card, and you hold that focus in that frontal lobe, let the yellow brain do the building and then move it back to midbrain to do the sending. You have got to get it out of the intellectual arena. No people are going to give this to you. It is not going to happen in any particular place. It is not connected to anything else. This is what you want and nothing similar. And it is not about time. And you have to make those orders very clear. It is Now. How many of you understand?

The object that you are focusing upon needs to be constructed from those things in your energy field, which is your reality, and it needs to be constructed out of those things that you do not have an attachment on but recognize. The greatest masters in the Great Work carry in their pockets or their purses three flat stones that go with them everywhere they go. And it is not as if they lost a stone that it could not be replaced. So those stones have no value to the master, but it is from these stones that the master turns them into gold coins. They are taking coagulated thought, releasing it, and re-forming it. And the three stones that they carry with them they got when their level of acceptance and their knowledge were ready to accept their capacity to do the work. So they have always carried the same three stones.

And herewith those of you who are serious about having no past and understand the metamorphosis of dissolutionment, you should carry with you in your pockets three insignificant things that as you are chattering idly, that your fingers are moving over their surfaces and that you are working them into that of value.

Before you go to your slumber, I want you to engage any part of the List you wish with this new understanding. Engage the List without people, places, things, times, and events. If you do, the List will become present. Got it? And you go to slumber with that on your mind. Got it? Now we are headed for exciting times. So sometime between now and six o'clock tomorrow morning, find your insignificant stuff. We have got to show you that it is a key to create out of and show you how to transform matter. That is the alchemist. Got it?

And did I tell you? Well, I love you, and I am so very happy we are in reunion together again because when we meet, we always progress. Thank God.

> O my Holy Spirit,
> I am upon you
> and you are within me.
> I am your outer shell.
> You are that which gives me life.
> Often I have felt
> like a meaningless puppet,
> wondering who pulls my strings
> and what part I shall play next.
> O my beloved Spirit,
> I tire of this play.
> I am weary of my uncontrolled destiny.
> O my Holy Spirit,
> I wish you to make me alive,
> aware, and powerful.
> I ask of you responsibility for my life.
> In this I desire
> to become my own immortal.
> O my beloved Spirit,
> dissolve my shell into you
> forever and ever and ever.
> So be it.
> To life.

I love you. Go in a happy Spirit. Remember everything I have taught you. Apply it. It works. And, above all, rejoice and be happy every day. Be grateful for this life, grateful that you are alive, grateful and privileged. And know that you are here for a reason and live to that reason's highest principle. So be it.

— *Ramtha*

RAMTHA'S GLOSSARY

Analogical. Being analogical means living in the Now. It is the creative moment and is outside of time, the past, and the emotions.

Analogical mind. Analogical mind means one mind. It is the result of the alignment of primary consciousness and secondary consciousness, the Observer and the personality. The fourth, fifth, sixth, and seventh seals of the body are opened in this state of mind. The bands spin in opposite directions, like a wheel within a wheel, creating a powerful vortex that allows the thoughts held in the frontal lobe to coagulate and manifest.

Bands, the. The bands are the two sets of seven frequencies that surround the human body and hold it together. Each of the seven frequency layers of each band corresponds to the seven seals of seven levels of consciousness in the human body. The bands are the auric field that allow the processes of binary and analogical mind.

Binary mind. This term means two minds. It is the mind produced by accessing the knowledge of the human personality and the physical body without accessing our deep subconscious mind. Binary mind relies solely on the knowledge, perception, and thought processes of the neocortex and the first three seals. The fourth, fifth, sixth, and seventh seals remain closed in this state of mind.

Blue Body®. It is the body that belongs to the fourth plane of existence, the bridge consciousness, and the ultraviolet frequency band. The Blue Body® is the lord over the lightbody and the physical plane.

Blue Body® Dance. It is a discipline taught by Ramtha in which the students lift their conscious awareness to the consciousness of the fourth plane. This discipline allows the Blue Body® to be accessed and the fourth seal to be opened.

Blue Body® Healing. It is a discipline taught by Ramtha in which the students lift their conscious awareness to the consciousness of the fourth plane and the Blue Body® for the purpose of healing or changing the physical body.

Blue webs. The blue webs represent the basic structure at a subtle level of the physical body. It is the invisible skeletal structure of the physical realm vibrating at the level of ultraviolet frequency.

Body/mind consciousness. Body/mind consciousness is the consciousness that belongs to the physical plane and the human body.

Book of Life. Ramtha refers to the soul as the Book of Life, where the whole journey of involution and evolution of each individual is recorded in the form of wisdom.

C&E® = R. Consciousness and energy create the nature of reality.

C&E®. Abbreviation of Consciousness & Energy℠. This is the service mark of the fundamental discipline of manifestation and the raising of consciousness taught in Ramtha's School of Enlightenment. Through this discipline the students learn to create an analogical state of mind, open up their higher seals, and create reality from the Void. A Beginning C&E® Workshop is the name of the Introductory Workshop for beginning students in which they learn the fundamental concepts and disciplines of Ramtha's teachings. The teachings of the Beginning C&E® Workshop can be found in *Ramtha, A Beginner's Guide to Creating Reality,* third ed. (Yelm: JZK Publishing, a division of JZK, Inc., 2004), and in *Ramtha, Creating Personal Reality*, Tape 380 ed. (Yelm: Ramtha Dialogues, 1998).

Christwalk. The Christwalk is a discipline designed by Ramtha in which the student learns to walk very slowly being acutely aware. In this discipline the students learn to manifest, with each step they take, the mind of a Christ.

Consciousness. Consciousness is the child who was born from the Void's contemplation of itself. It is the essence and fabric of all being. Everything that exists originated in consciousness and manifested outwardly through its handmaiden energy. A stream of consciousness refers to the continuum of the mind of God.

Consciousness and energy. Consciousness and energy are the dynamic force of creation and are inextricably combined. Everything that exists originated in consciousness and manifested through the modulation of its energy impact into mass.

Create Your Day^{SM}. This is the service mark for a technique created by Ramtha for raising consciousness and energy and intentionally creating a constructive plan of experiences and events for the day early in the morning before the start of the day. This technique is exclusively taught at Ramtha's School of Enlightenment.

Disciplines of the Great Work. Ramtha's School of Ancient Wisdom is dedicated to the Great Work. The disciplines of the Great Work practiced in Ramtha's School of Enlightenment are all designed in their entirety by Ramtha. These practices are powerful initiations where the student has the opportunity to apply and experience firsthand the teachings of Ramtha.

Emotional body. The emotional body is the collection of past emotions, attitudes, and electrochemical patterns that make up the brain's neuronet and define the human personality of an individual. Ramtha describes it as the seduction of the unenlightened. It is the reason for cyclical reincarnation.

Emotions. An emotion is the physical, biochemical effect of an experience. Emotions belong to the past, for they are the expression of experiences that are already known and mapped in the neuropathways of the brain.

Energy. Energy is the counterpart of consciousness. All consciousness carries with it a dynamic energy impact, radiation, or natural expression of itself. Likewise, all forms of energy carry with it a consciousness that defines it.

Enlightenment. Enlightenment is the full realization of the human person, the attainment of immortality, and unlimited mind. It is the result of raising the kundalini energy sitting at the base of the spine to the seventh seal that opens the dormant parts of the brain. When the energy penetrates the lower cerebellum and the midbrain, and the subconscious mind is opened, the individual experiences a blinding flash of light called enlightenment.

Evolution. Evolution is the journey back home from the slowest levels of frequency and mass to the highest levels of consciousness and Point Zero.

Fieldwork^{SM}. Fieldwork^{SM} is one of the fundamental disciplines of Ramtha's School of Enlightenment. The students are taught to create a symbol of something they want to know and experience and draw it on a paper card. These cards are placed with the blank side facing out on the fence rails of a large field. The students blindfold themselves and focus on their symbol, allowing their body to walk freely to find their card through the application of the law of consciousness and energy and analogical mind.

Fifth plane. The fifth plane of existence is the plane of superconsciousness and x-ray frequency. It is also known as the Golden Plane or paradise.

Fifth seal. This seal is the center of our spiritual body that connects us to the fifth plane. It is associated with the thyroid gland and with speaking and living the truth without dualism.

First plane. It refers to the material or physical plane. It is the plane of the image consciousness and Hertzian frequency. It is the slowest and densest form of coagulated consciousness and energy.

First seal. The first seal is associated with the reproductive organs, sexuality, and survival.

First three seals. The first three seals are the seals of sexuality, pain and suffering, and controlling power. These are the seals commonly at play in all of the complexities of the human drama.

Fourth plane. The fourth plane of existence is the realm of the bridge consciousness and ultraviolet frequency. This plane is described as the plane of Shiva, the destroyer of the old and creator of the new. In this plane, energy is not yet split into positive and negative polarity. Any lasting changes or healing of the physical body must be changed first at the level of the fourth plane and the Blue Body®. This plane is also called the Blue Plane, or the plane of Shiva.

Fourth seal. The fourth seal is associated with unconditional love and the thymus gland. When this seal is activated, a hormone is released that maintains the body in perfect health and stops the aging process.

God. Ramtha's teachings are an exposition of the statement, "You are God." Humanity is described as the forgotten Gods, divine beings by nature who have forgotten their heritage and true identity. It is precisely this statement that represents Ramtha's challenging message to our modern age, an age riddled with religious superstition and misconceptions about the divine and the true knowledge of wisdom.

God within. It is the Observer, the great self, the primary consciousness, the Spirit, the God within the human person.

God/man. The full realization of a human being.

God/woman. The full realization of a human being.

Gods. The Gods are technologically advanced beings from other star systems who came to Earth 455,000 years ago. These Gods manipulated the human race genetically, mixing and modifying our DNA with theirs. They are responsible for the evolution of the neocortex and used the human race as a subdued work force. Evidence of these events is recorded in the Sumerian tablets and artifacts. This term is also used to describe the true identity of humanity, the forgotten Gods.

Golden body. It is the body that belongs to the fifth plane, superconsciousness, and x-ray frequency.

Great Work. The Great Work is the practical application of the knowledge of the Schools of Ancient Wisdom. It refers to the disciplines by which the human person becomes enlightened and is transmuted into an immortal, divine being.

Grid^{SM}, The. This is the service mark for a technique created by Ramtha for raising consciousness and energy and intentionally tapping into the Zero Point Energy field and the fabric of reality through a mental visualization. This technique is exclusively taught at Ramtha's School of Enlightenment.

Hierophant. A hierophant is a master teacher who is able to manifest what they teach and initiate their students into such knowledge.

Hyperconsciousness. Hyperconsciousness is the consciousness of the sixth plane and gamma ray frequency.

Infinite Unknown. It is the frequency band of the seventh plane of existence and ultraconsciousness.

Involution. Involution is the journey from Point Zero and the seventh plane to the slowest and densest levels of frequency and mass.

JZ Knight. JZ Knight is the only person appointed by Ramtha to channel him. Ramtha refers to JZ as his beloved daughter. She was Ramaya, the eldest of the children given to Ramtha during his lifetime.

Kundalini. Kundalini energy is the life force of a person that descends from the higher seals to the base of the spine at puberty. It is a large packet of energy reserved for human evolution, commonly pictured as a coiled serpent that sits at the base of the spine. This energy is different from the energy coming out of the first three seals responsible for sexuality, pain and suffering, power, and victimization. It is commonly described as the sleeping serpent or the sleeping dragon. The journey of the kundalini energy to the crown of the head is called the journey of enlightenment. This journey takes place when this serpent wakes up and starts to split and dance around the spine, ionizing the spinal fluid and changing its molecular structure. This action causes the opening of the midbrain and the door to the subconscious mind.

Life force. The life force is the Father/Mother, the Spirit, the breath of life within the person that is the platform from which the person creates its illusions, imagination, and dreams.

Life review. It is the review of the previous incarnation that occurs when the person reaches the third plane after death. The person gets the opportunity to be the Observer, the actor, and the recipient of its own actions. The unresolved issues from that lifetime that emerge at the life or light review set the agenda for the next incarnation.

Light, the. The light refers to the third plane of existence.

Lightbody. It is the same as the radiant body. It is the body that belongs to the third plane of conscious awareness and the visible light frequency band.

List, the. The List is the discipline taught by Ramtha where the student gets to write a list of items they desire to know and experience and then learn to focus on it in an analogical state of consciousness. The List is the map used to design, change, and reprogram the neuronet of the person. It is the tool that helps to bring meaningful and lasting changes in the person and their reality.

Make known the unknown. This phrase expresses the original divine mandate given to the Source consciousness to manifest and bring to conscious awareness all of the infinite potentials of the Void. This statement represents the basic intent that inspires the dynamic process of creation and evolution.

Mind. Mind is the product of streams of consciousness and energy acting on the brain creating thought-forms, holographic segments, or neurosynaptic patterns called memory. The streams of consciousness and energy are what keep the brain alive. They are its power source. A person's ability to think is what gives them a mind.

Mind of God. The mind of God comprises the mind and wisdom of every lifeform that ever lived on any dimension, in any time, or that ever will live on any planet, any star, or region of space.

Mirror consciousness. When Point Zero imitated the act of contemplation of the Void it created a mirror reflection of itself, a point of reference that made the exploration of the Void possible. It is called mirror consciousness or secondary consciousness. See **Self.**

Monkey-mind. Monkey-mind refers to the flickering, swinging mind of the personality.

Mother/Father Principle. It is the source of all life, the Father, the eternal Mother, the Void. In Ramtha's teachings, the Source and God the creator are not the same. God the creator is seen as Point Zero and primary consciousness but not as the Source, or the Void, itself.

Name-field. The name-field is the name of the large field where the discipline of Fieldwork^SM is practiced.

Neighborhood Walk^SM. This is the service mark of a technique created by JZ Knight for raising consciousness and energy and intentionally modifying our neuronets and set patterns of thinking no longer wanted and replacing them with new ones of our choice. This technique is exclusively taught at Ramtha's School of Enlightenment.

Neuronet. The contraction for "neural network," a network of neurons that perform a function together.

Observer. It refers to the Observer responsible for collapsing the particle/wave of quantum mechanics. It represents the great self, the Spirit, primary consciousness, the God within the human person.

Outrageous. Ramtha uses this word in a positive way to express something or someone who is extraordinary and unusual, unrestrained in action, and excessively bold or fierce.

People, places, things, times, and events. These are the main areas of human experience to which the personality is emotionally attached. These areas represent the past of the human person and constitute the content of the emotional body.

Personality, the. See **Emotional body.**

Plane of Bliss. It refers to the plane of rest where souls get to plan their next incarnations after their life reviews. It is also known as heaven and paradise where there is no suffering, no pain, no need or lack, and where every wish is immediately manifested.

Plane of demonstration. The physical plane is also called the plane of demonstration. It is the plane where the person has the opportunity to demonstrate its creative potentiality in mass and witness consciousness in material form in order to expand its emotional understanding.

Point Zero. It refers to the original point of awareness created by the Void through its act of contemplating itself. Point Zero is the original child of the Void, the birth of consciousness.

Primary consciousness. It is the Observer, the great self, the God within the human person.

Ram. Ram is a shorter version of the name Ramtha. Ramtha means the Father.

Ramaya. Ramtha refers to JZ Knight as his beloved daughter. She was Ramaya, the first one to become Ramtha's adopted child during his lifetime. Ramtha found Ramaya abandoned on the steppes of Russia. Many people gave their children to Ramtha during the march as a gesture of love and highest respect; these children were to be raised in the House of the Ram. His children grew to the great number of 133 even though he never had offspring of his own blood.

Ramtha (etymology). The name of Ramtha the Enlightened One, Lord of the Wind, means the Father. It also refers to the Ram who descended from the mountain on what is known as the terrible day of the Ram. "It is about that in all antiquity. And in ancient Egypt, there is an avenue dedicated to the Ram, the great conqueror. And they were wise enough to understand that whoever could walk down the avenue of the Ram could conquer the wind." The word Aram, the name of Noah's grandson, is formed from the Aramaic noun Araa — meaning earth, landmass — and the word Ramtha, meaning high. This Semitic name echoes Ramtha's descent from the high mountain, which began the great march.

Runner. A runner in Ramtha's lifetime was responsible for bringing specific messages or information. A master teacher has the ability to send runners to other people that manifest their words or intent in the form of an experience or an event.

Second plane. It is the plane of existence of social consciousness and the infrared frequency band. It is associated with pain and suffering. This plane is the negative polarity of the third plane of visible light frequency.

Second seal. This seal is the energy center of social consciousness and the infrared frequency band. It is associated with the experience of pain and suffering and is located in the lower abdominal area.

Secondary consciousness. When Point Zero imitated the act of contemplation of the Void it created a mirror reflection of itself, a point of reference that made the exploration of the Void possible. It is called mirror consciousness or secondary consciousness. *See* **Self.**

Self, the. The self is the true identity of the human person different from the personality. It is the transcendental aspect of the person. It refers to the secondary consciousness, the traveler in a journey of involution and evolution making known the unknown.

Sending-and-receiving. Sending-and-receiving is the name of the discipline taught by Ramtha in which the student learns to access information using the faculties of the midbrain to the exclusion of sensory perception. This discipline develops the student's psychic ability of telepathy and divination.

Seven seals. The seven seals are powerful energy centers that constitute seven levels of consciousness in the human body. The bands are the way in which the physical body is held together according to these seals. In every human being there is energy spiraling out of the first three seals or centers. The energy pulsating out of the first three seals manifests itself respectively as sexuality, pain, or power. When the upper seals are unlocked, a higher level of awareness is activated.

Seventh plane. The seventh plane is the plane of ultraconsciousness and the Infinite Unknown frequency band. This plane is where the journey of involution began. This plane was created by Point Zero when it imitated the act of contemplation of the Void and the mirror or secondary consciousness was created. A plane of existence or dimension of space and time exists between two points of consciousness. All the other planes were created by slowing down the time and frequency band of the seventh plane.

Seventh seal. This seal is associated with the crown of the head, the pituitary gland, and the attainment of enlightenment.

Shiva. The Lord God Shiva represents the Lord of the Blue Plane and the Blue Body®. Shiva is not used in reference to a singular deity from Hinduism. It is rather the representation of a state of consciousness that belongs to the fourth plane, the ultraviolet frequency band, and the opening of the fourth seal. Shiva is neither male nor female. It is an androgynous being, for the energy of the fourth plane has not yet been split into positive and negative polarity. This is an important distinction from the traditional Hindu representation of Shiva as a male deity who has a wife. The tiger skin at its feet, the trident staff, and the sun and the moon at the level of the head represent the mastery of this body over the first three seals of consciousness. The kundalini energy is pictured as fiery energy shooting from the base of the spine through the head. This is another distinction from some Hindu representations of Shiva with the serpent energy coming out at the level of the fifth seal or throat. Another symbolic image of Shiva is the long threads of dark hair and an abundance of pearl necklaces, which represent its richness of experience owned into wisdom. The quiver and bow and arrows are the agent by which Shiva shoots its powerful will and destroys imperfection and creates the new.

Sixth plane. The sixth plane is the realm of hyperconsciousness and the gamma ray frequency band. In this plane the awareness of being one with the whole of life is experienced.

Sixth seal. This seal is associated with the pineal gland and the gamma ray frequency band. The reticular formation that filters and veils the knowingness of the subconscious mind is opened when this seal is activated. The opening of the brain refers to the opening of this seal and the activation of its consciousness and energy.

Social consciousness. It is the consciousness of the second plane and the infrared frequency band. It is also called the image of the human personality and the mind of the first three seals. Social consciousness refers to the collective consciousness of human society. It is the collection of thoughts, assumptions, judgments, prejudices, laws, morality, values, attitudes, ideals, and emotions of the fraternity of the human race.

Soul. Ramtha refers to the soul as the Book of Life, where the whole journey of involution and evolution of the individual is recorded in the form of wisdom.

Subconscious mind. The seat of the subconscious mind is the lower cerebellum or reptilian brain. This part of the brain has its own independent connections to the frontal lobe and the whole of the body and has the power to access the mind of God, the wisdom of the ages.

Superconsciousness. This is the consciousness of the fifth plane and the x-ray frequency band.

Tahumo. Tahumo is the discipline taught by Ramtha in which the student learns the ability to master the effects of the natural environment — cold and heat — on the human body.

Tank field. It is the name of the large field with the labyrinth that is used for the discipline of The Tank®.

Tank®, The. It is the name given to the labyrinth used as part of the disciplines of Ramtha's School of Enlightenment. The students are taught to find the entry to this labyrinth blindfolded and move through it focusing on the Void without touching the walls or using the eyes or the senses. The objective of this discipline is to find, blindfolded, the center of the labyrinth or a room designated and representative of the Void.

Third plane. This is the plane of conscious awareness and the visible light frequency band. It is also known as the light plane and the mental plane. When the energy of the Blue Plane is lowered down to this frequency band, it splits into positive and negative polarity. It is at this point that the soul splits into two, giving origin to the phenomenon of soulmates.

Third seal. This seal is the energy center of conscious awareness and the visible light frequency band. It is associated with control, tyranny, victimization, and power. It is located in the region of the solar plexus.

Thought. Thought is different from consciousness. The brain processes a stream of consciousness, modifying it into segments — holographic pictures — of neurological, electrical, and chemical prints called thoughts. Thoughts are the building blocks of mind.

Torsion Process^{SM}. This is the service mark of a technique created by Ramtha for raising consciousness and energy and intentionally creating a torsion field using the mind. Through this technique the student learns to build a wormhole in space/time, alter reality, and create dimensional phenomena such as invisibility, levitation, bilocation, teleportation, and others. This technique is exclusively taught at Ramtha's School of Enlightenment.

Twilight®. This term is used to describe the discipline taught by Ramtha in which the students learn to put their bodies in a catatonic state similar to deep sleep, yet retaining their conscious awareness.

Twilight® Visualization Process. It is the process used to practice the discipline of the List or other visualization formats.

Ultraconsciousness. It is the consciousness of the seventh plane and the Infinite Unknown frequency band. It is the consciousness of an ascended master.

Unknown God. The Unknown God was the single God of Ramtha's ancestors, the Lemurians. The Unknown God also represents the forgotten divinity and divine origin of the human person.

Upper four seals. The upper four seals are the fourth, fifth, sixth, and seventh seals.

Void, the. The Void is defined as one vast nothing materially, yet all things potentially. See **Mother/Father Principle.**

Yellow brain. The yellow brain is Ramtha's name for the neocortex, the house of analytical and emotional thought. The reason why it is called the yellow brain is because the neocortices were colored yellow in the original two-dimensional, caricature-style drawing Ramtha used for his teaching on the function of the brain and its processes. He explained that the different aspects of the brain in this particular drawing are exaggerated and colorfully highlighted for the sake of study and understanding. This specific drawing became the standard tool used in all the subsequent teachings on the brain.

Yeshua ben Joseph. Ramtha refers to Jesus Christ by the name Yeshua ben Joseph, following the Jewish traditions of that time.

Fig. A: The Seven Seals:
Seven Levels of Consciousness in the Human Body

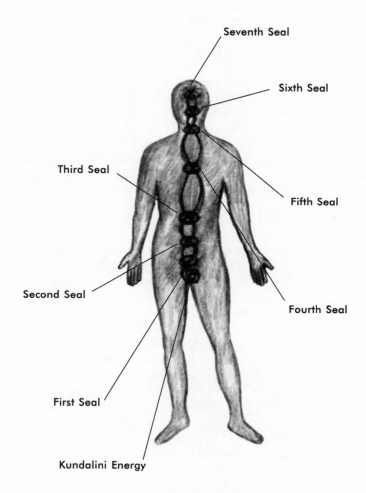

Seventh Seal

Sixth Seal

Third Seal

Fifth Seal

Second Seal

Fourth Seal

First Seal

Kundalini Energy

FIG. B: SEVEN LEVELS OF CONSCIOUSNESS AND ENERGY

Point Zero

Ultraconsciousness	7	Infinite Unknown
Hyperconsciousness	6	Gamma Ray
Superconsciousness	5	X-Ray
Bridge Consciousness	4	Ultraviolet Blue
Conscious Awareness	3	Visible Light
Social Consciousness	2	Infrared
Subconsciousness	1	Hertzian

The Now

Copyright © 2000 JZ Knight

FIG. C: SEVEN BODIES ENFOLDED WITHIN EACH OTHER

Point Zero

7th Level
6th Level
5th Level
4th Level
3rd Level
2nd Level
1st Level

Copyright © 2000 JZ Knight

Fig. D: Consciousness and Energy in the Light Spectrum

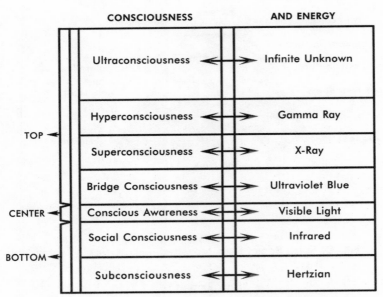

Copyright © 2000 JZ Knight

FIG. E: THE BRAIN

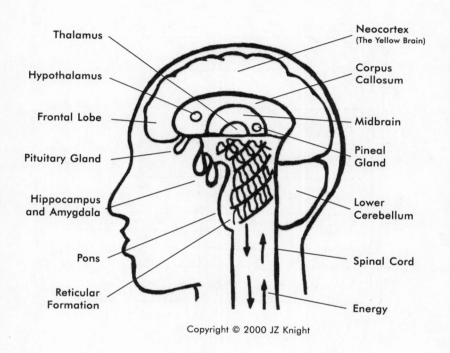

Thalamus

Hypothalamus

Frontal Lobe

Pituitary Gland

Hippocampus
and Amygdala

Pons

Reticular
Formation

Neocortex
(The Yellow Brain)

Corpus
Callosum

Midbrain

Pineal
Gland

Lower
Cerebellum

Spinal Cord

Energy

Copyright © 2000 JZ Knight

This is the original two-dimensional caricature-style drawing Ramtha used for his teaching on the function of the brain and its processes. He explained that the different aspects of the brain in this particular drawing are exaggerated and colorfully highlighted for the sake of study and understanding. This specific drawing became the standard tool used in all the subsequent teachings on the brain.

Fig. F: Binary Mind — Living the Image

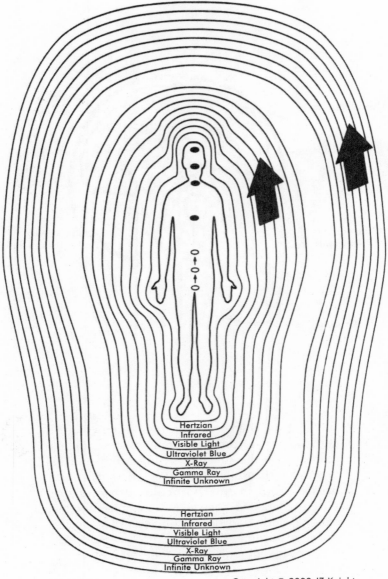

Hertzian
Infrared
Visible Light
Ultraviolet Blue
X-Ray
Gamma Ray
Infinite Unknown

Hertzian
Infrared
Visible Light
Ultraviolet Blue
X-Ray
Gamma Ray
Infinite Unknown

FIG. G: ANALOGICAL MIND — LIVING IN THE NOW

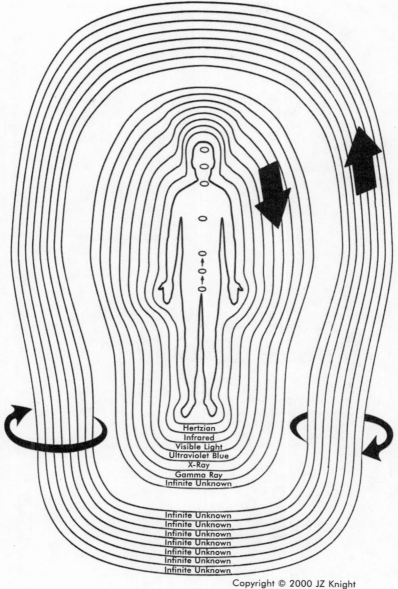

Hertzian
Infrared
Visible Light
Ultraviolet Blue
X-Ray
Gamma Ray
Infinite Unknown

Infinite Unknown
Infinite Unknown
Infinite Unknown
Infinite Unknown
Infinite Unknown
Infinite Unknown
Infinite Unknown

Fig. H: The Observer Effect and the Nerve Cell

The Observer is responsible
for collapsing the wave function of probability
into particle reality.

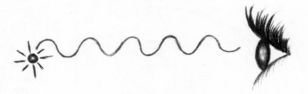

Particle   Energy wave   The Observer

The act of observation
makes the nerve cells fire and produces thought.

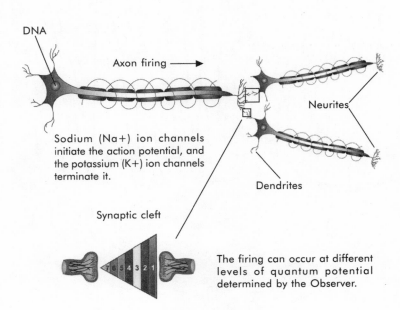

DNA

Axon firing ⟶

Neurites

Sodium (Na+) ion channels
initiate the action potential, and
the potassium (K+) ion channels
terminate it.

Dendrites

Synaptic cleft

The firing can occur at different
levels of quantum potential
determined by the Observer.

Fig. 1: Cellular Biology and the Thought Connection

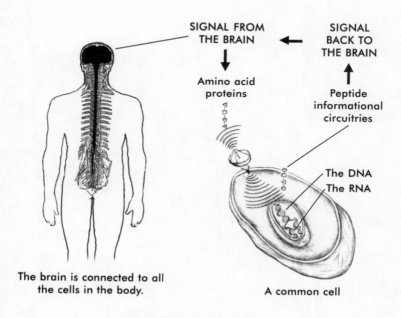

SIGNAL FROM
THE BRAIN

SIGNAL
BACK TO
THE BRAIN

Amino acid
proteins

Peptide
informational
circuitries

The DNA
The RNA

The brain is connected to all
the cells in the body.

A common cell

Ramtha's School of Enlightenment
THE SCHOOL OF ANCIENT WISDOM

A Division of JZK, Inc.
P.O. Box 1210
Yelm, Washington 98597
360.458.5201
800.347.0439
www.ramtha.com
www.jzkpublishing.com